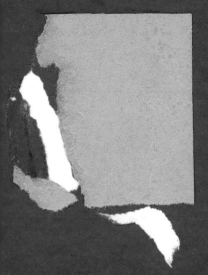

GROWING UP IN WORLD WAR TWO

ENTERTAINMENT

Catherine Burch

FRANKLIN WATTS
LONDON•SYDNEY

First published in 2005
by Franklin Watts
96 Leonard Street, London
EC2A 4XD

Franklin Watts Australia
Level 17/207 Kent Street,
Sydney, NSW 2000

© 2005 Franklin Watts

Produced for Franklin Watts by
White-Thomson Publishing Ltd,
Bridgewater Business Centre, 210 High Street, Lewes,
East Sussex BN7 2NH

Consultant: Andrew Spooner, military historian
Design: Bernard Higton Design
Picture acknowledgements: All photographs courtesy
of Getty Images–Hulton Archive.

A CIP catalogue record for this book is available from
the British Library.

ISBN 0 7496 6197 6

Dewey classification number: 790'.0941'09044

Printed in China

CONTENTS

Words in the glossary are in **bold** the first time they appear in the text.

KEEP SMILING THROUGH

Daily life in Britain was very difficult during World War Two (1939–1945). Thousands of people's homes were destroyed by bombs, and ordinary civilians were killed.

Several million children and others were **evacuated** from their homes to safer areas. It was difficult to buy many everyday things that people needed, like food and clothes. Yet many people remember the war as a good time when everyone helped each other. The words of a popular song were, 'Keep smiling through'. People were glad to be alive and they laughed about their troubles.

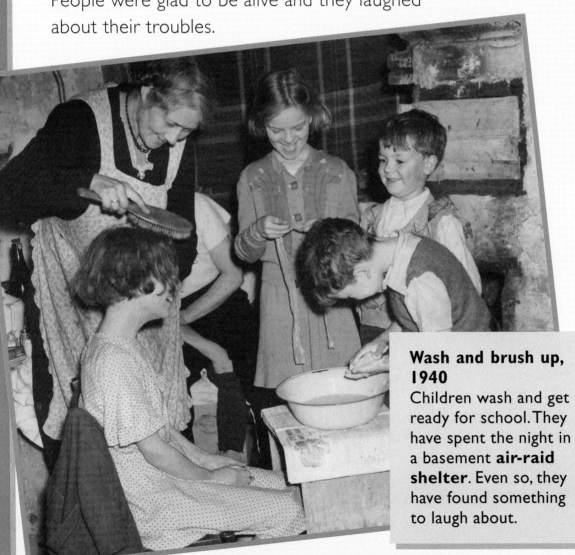

Wash and brush up, 1940
Children wash and get ready for school. They have spent the night in a basement **air-raid shelter**. Even so, they have found something to laugh about.

Talking with neighbours, 1941
Women chat over the garden fence, wearing **gas masks**. Everyone knew their neighbours and shared each other's troubles.

Have a cuppa, 1940
After **air raids**, vans went round handing out hot food and drinks to comfort people.

CINEMA-GOERS

Television had only just been invented when the war started and programmes were stopped during the war. Computers, videos and DVDs had not been invented.

Instead of watching television, children loved going to the cinema. Most adults and children went at least once a week, especially those who lived in towns. Once you had paid to go in, you could stay as long as you liked and watch the same film over again. Cinemas showed **news reels**, as well as films.

Film fans, 1940
Children watch an afternoon film. Cinemas had huge screens and were always packed. They kept hundreds of thousands of children entertained.

Queuing for a seat, 1944
People wait in long queues for the cinema. For a while, some cinemas let people stay all night.

Glittering Grable, 1945
The film star, Betty Grable. Film stars helped people forget the troubles of war for a while.

WIRELESS

At home people listened to the wireless (or radio, as we call it now) every day. The wireless was as important to people then as television is today.

Families sat round together in the evening to listen to the news about the war. Everyone wanted to hear what was going on, especially if a member of the family was away fighting somewhere. Music and **comedy shows** on the wireless lifted people's spirits. There were a few programmes for children, such as *Children's Hour*.

It's That Man Again, 1945
One popular radio show was called *ITMA*, or *It's That Man Again*. It made children and adults laugh all through the war. Here, the *ITMA* team makes one of their programmes.

Listening to Churchill, 1941
Londoners sit in a pub, listening to a speech on the radio by the British prime minister, Winston Churchill. His speeches helped to make people feel stronger.

I REMEMBER ························
'It seems that most of my time was spent listening to songs on the radio, and memorising them.'
········ (Iris Horne, from BBC WW2 People's War website)

AIR-RAID ENTERTAINMENT

At times, German planes attacked Britain night after night. People had to spend many hours in air-raid shelters, which was boring, uncomfortable, tiring and often frightening.

People tried to keep cheerful during air raids by telling jokes, playing games, singing and putting on concerts. Some people preferred to shelter in church halls and evacuated schools. Someone would play the piano loudly to drown out the sound of planes overhead. There was often someone selling refreshments so that people did not go hungry.

Dominoes by candlelight, 1939
A family plays dominoes in its shelter during an air raid. Lots of families built air-raid shelters in their back gardens.

Underground sounds, 1940

Hundreds of people, crowded into a London underground train station for shelter, watch a concert. Entertainments like this one helped people to forget their fears for a while.

SINGING AND DANCING

Singing and dancing were very popular during the war. At weekends dance halls were full of people dancing to the music of big bands. Women often danced together because so many men were away at war.

Young women worked hard on farms or in factories to help the war effort during the week. They looked forward to having fun at a dance on a Saturday night. Popular singers, such as Vera Lynn, sang songs that helped cheer people up when they were missing their loved ones.

Tea with Vera, 1942
Here the singer, Vera Lynn, opens a mobile canteen. She was known as the 'Forces' Sweetheart', because she was so popular with young men away at war. She gave them hope with songs like *We'll Meet Again*.

'Don't Dilly Dally On The Way', 1944 Boys from Chelsea Boys' Club sing together around a piano. Most people knew the words to popular songs.

I REMEMBER ....

'Our house had a very large cellar, and this is where we... took shelter during the many air raids... the many nights spent in the cellar became more party-like... I remember home-made ginger beer, flasks of tea, sandwiches and, most of all, everyone singing!'

(Iris Horne, from BBC WW2 People's War website)

THEATRE

Theatres and cinemas were closed for a few weeks at the beginning of the war. The government thought it was too dangerous to have lots of people together in case a bomb fell on the theatre. But the government soon realised it was important to keep people feeling cheerful and hopeful.

Going to the theatre was a treat for children and adults. Pantomimes, puppet shows and magicians were popular with children. Villages put on their own plays and shows.

Winning talent, 1940
The winner of a talent competition at a street party. Children took part in singing and dancing competitions, hoping to be famous one day.

Clowning around, 1943
A clown show in a London park entertains children during their school holidays. People went to live performances more often than we do today, probably because there were no televisions, videos or DVDs.

TOY SHORTAGES

There were shortages of everything in the shops, including food, clothes and toys. German U-boats attacked and sank ships carrying supplies to Britain from other countries.

Dolls were rare. Not so many books were published, and newspapers had fewer pages because there was a shortage of paper. Factories made very few bicycles and metal toys. Nearly all Britain's metal was used to make guns, tanks and planes.

Keen readers, 1940
Boys huddle together to read the latest story in their comic. Not many comics were printed, so children often had to share with their friends.

A precious doll, 1940
A little girl sits in a bomb-site, cuddling her precious doll. Her home was damaged by a bomb but luckily she was not hurt.

I REMEMBER.............................
'Went Christmas shopping yesterday... toys were very difficult. Metal toys are practically non-existent... I wish I could have bought a railway train for my boy.'
●●●●●●●●●●●●●● *(Mr Brown's War, A Diary of the Second World War)*

MAKE DO AND MEND

You could not buy many toys in shops so a lot of people made their own. Before birthdays and Christmas, many parents spent their evenings making toys to give to their children.

Home-made ragdolls were common, and so were war-like toys – aeroplanes, tanks and guns made from wood. Some people made beautiful dolls' houses. There were not many new bicycles for sale in the shops, but sometimes people could make one out of parts from old bikes.

I REMEMBER........

'My cousin Jenny lived next door. We each had a swing made from rope and a wooden seat, made by our fathers, which hung from hooks inside the back door. We spent hours in the summer trying to swing in time together.'

.... (Kate, Bristol)

Propeller problems, 1941
A boy struggles to fit the propeller onto the nose of his home-made model aircraft.

Christmas underground, 1940
An air-raid warden decorates an underground shelter. The decorations must have been made before the war, as paper was scarce. You had to take your own bags to shops to wrap up what you bought.

Get well soon, 1940
A boy plays draughts with a nurse in hospital. He was injured in an air raid. Simple, **traditional** games like draughts and chess were popular and easy to make.

SALVAGE AND TROPHIES

Factories desperately needed metal to make planes, guns and other war supplies. People collected anything made of metal that was not needed and sent it to factories. This was known as 'salvage'.

Bits of wrecked planes, old saucepans, baths and bikes were all taken to the salvage dump. Children enjoyed collecting salvage. There was even a national club called 'Cogs' to encourage them. Children also liked hunting for bits of bombs and crashed planes. They competed to see who had the best collection of 'trophies'.

'Be a dumper', 1940
Children dump old toys onto a salvage heap. The government asked people to throw away old metal things they no longer needed.

I REMEMBER ....

'Once a German plane crashed near the road to Offham. We rushed off to grab bits for our collection and when we got there the dead pilot was still in his seat. I remember thinking how small the plane was, but maybe this was because the tail half had broken off.'

(Sheila, Lewes)

Bath boy, 1939
A little boy carries an old metal bath to the salvage dump.

Wreckage collectors, 1941
Boys salvage parts of a German plane that crashed on the south coast.

HOLIDAYS

Not everyone could afford to go on holiday in the 1940s. Many people just went on day trips. It was especially difficult to take holidays during the war.

There were barbed wire defences on a lot of beaches on the south and east coasts of England, in case the enemy tried to invade. People went on holiday to 'safe' areas, such as Devon or Blackpool. Everyone had to travel by train or bus. **Petrol rationing** meant there was no petrol for family cars.

Blackpool beach, 1943
A soldier makes a sandcastle for his granddaughter. There were no ice-creams for holidaymakers on the beach during the war.

Donkey riders, 1943
Children on a beach in Blackpool enjoy a donkey ride.

I REMEMBER...

'The first time I ever went further than Brighton was on a Sunday School day trip to Littlehampton. We were allowed to go in the sea, but everyone laughed at me because of the dreadful little petticoat I was wearing. My mother used to make me petticoats from the parachutes attached to incendiary bombs that we picked up when walking on the Downs.'

(Sheila, Lewes)

THE GIs

The USA joined the war in 1941. Thousands of US soldiers and airmen came to Britain to get ready for going to fight Germany. US troops were known as GIs.

The GIs seemed different and exciting. They had things that were scarce in Britain, like chocolate, cigarettes, scented soap and nylon stockings. They gave these away and made themselves very popular. They brought fun new things to Britain, like Coca-Cola, chewing gum and lively new dances, such as the jitterbug.

Party time, 1942
GIs give a party for children who have suffered during the war. Children especially loved the GIs, who gave them sweets and chewing gum.

Swing crazy, 1945
A club for US **servicemen**.
Here they could drink Coca-Cola, play **pool** and dance.
British women liked going to the dances they held.

I REMEMBER ....

'... The American forces... were pestered for chewing gum and were usually generous – they were much better paid and supplied than our forces.'

.... (John Heathcote, from BBC WW2 People's War website)

SPORT

The government cancelled all football matches at the start of the war. It thought it was too dangerous for big crowds to gather, in case a bomb dropped on them. But matches soon began again because they were so important for keeping people cheerful.

Many sports carried on, but there were fewer teams than usual because many men were away fighting the war. A lot of football pitches, cricket grounds, racecourses and playing fields were taken over. The army used some, and others were dug up for **allotments** for growing food. The famous cricket ground in London, called the Oval, became a **prisoner-of-war camp**.

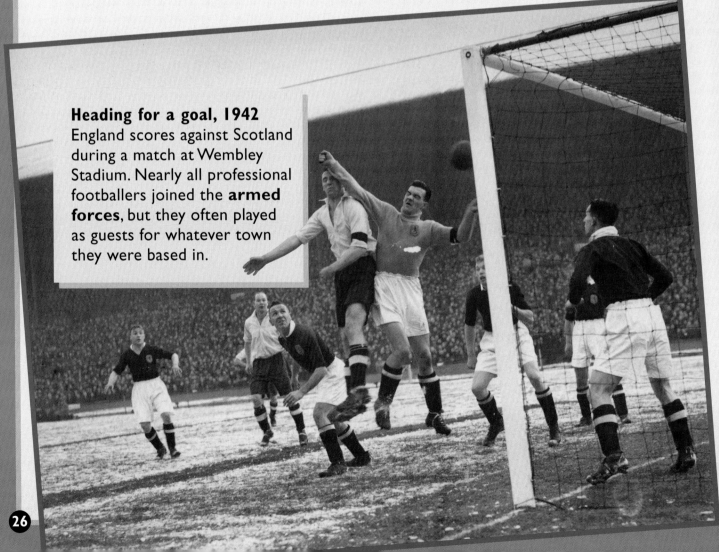

Heading for a goal, 1942
England scores against Scotland during a match at Wembley Stadium. Nearly all professional footballers joined the **armed forces**, but they often played as guests for whatever town they were based in.

Wartime racing, 1940
Some horse-racing carried on during the war. Here, airmen enjoy the races at the famous racecourse at Newmarket.

Tough tackle, 1943
Children play football. Football boots and footballs were in short supply in shops.

THE END OF THE WAR

The war in Europe ended when Germany surrendered in May 1945. All over Britain people celebrated wildly. In London, searchlights lit up the night sky and huge crowds sang and danced on the streets. In other towns, church bells rang out and fireworks flashed for the first time since war began.

Television programmes began to be shown again in June 1946, a year after the war ended. Many people bought their first television set in 1953 to be able to watch the Queen's **Coronation**. About 22 million people watched it on television.

Let's party, May 1945
To celebrate VE (Victory in Europe) Day, people held street parties. Everyone brought something to eat and drink.

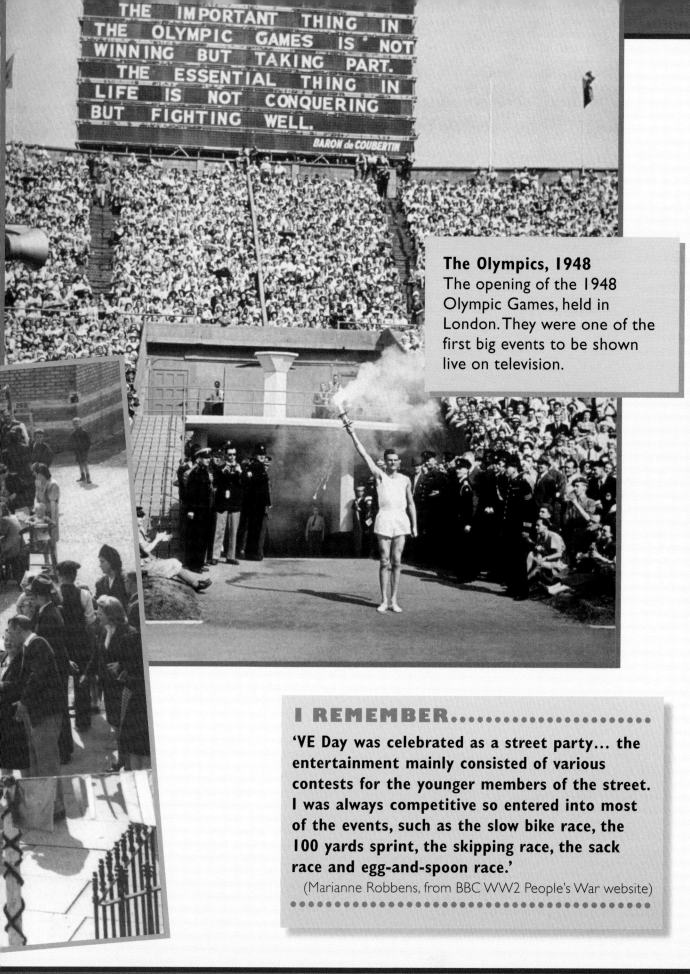

THE IMPORTANT THING IN THE OLYMPIC GAMES IS NOT WINNING BUT TAKING PART. THE ESSENTIAL THING IN LIFE IS NOT CONQUERING BUT FIGHTING WELL.

BARON de COUBERTIN

The Olympics, 1948
The opening of the 1948 Olympic Games, held in London. They were one of the first big events to be shown live on television.

I REMEMBER......................

'VE Day was celebrated as a street party... the entertainment mainly consisted of various contests for the younger members of the street. I was always competitive so entered into most of the events, such as the slow bike race, the 100 yards sprint, the skipping race, the sack race and egg-and-spoon race.'

(Marianne Robbens, from BBC WW2 People's War website)

GLOSSARY

Air raid sudden attack by planes dropping bombs, such as the nightly attacks on Britain by German planes during the Blitz

Air-raid shelters safe places to go during an air raid, when German planes were dropping bombs

Allotments areas of land in villages or towns to use for growing things, such as fruit and vegetables

Armed forces the forces to protect a country: its army, air force and navy

Civilians members of the public, not of the army, navy or air force

Comedy shows programmes that make fun of things, to make you laugh

Coronation the ceremony when a king or queen is crowned

Downs the chalk hills in southern England

Evacuated sent away for safety. Some people, such as children, mothers with babies, people with disabilities and the long-term sick, who lived in the most dangerous areas, were sent to live in a safer place.

Gas masks masks that allow people to breathe without being poisoned if there is gas in the air. At the beginning of the war, everyone had to carry a gas mask in case the enemy dropped bombs with poison gas in them.

GIs members of the US army and air force were known as GIs in Britain, because they all wore uniforms with GI on them, standing for 'General Issue'.

Incendiary bombs bombs designed to catch fire when they land. They didn't always work.

News reels short films that showed real-life news events in the days before television

Petrol rationing only giving a certain amount of petrol to people, such as lorry drivers and farmers, who really needed it. Petrol had to be shipped from abroad, so it was in short supply.

Petticoat an underskirt that women and girls wore under their top skirt

Pool game played with coloured balls on a table. Each player has to hit their balls into pockets on the table.

Prisoner-of-war camp enemy soldiers who were captured were called prisoners-of-war and were kept in special prison camps

Servicemen men who are in the 'services' – the army, navy and air force

Traditional describes something that is handed down from one generation to another, like songs, games and customs

U-boats German submarines

FURTHER INFORMATION

Books

Butterfield, Moira, *Going to War in World War Two* (Franklin Watts, 2001)

Cooper, Alison, *Rationing* (Hodder Wayland, 2003)

Deary, Terry, *Horrible History, The Woeful Second World War* (Hippo, 1999)

Hamley, Dennis, *The Second World War* (Franklin Watts, 2004)

Masters, Anthony, *World War II Stories* (Franklin Watts, 2004)

Parsons, Martin, *Britain at War: Rationing* (Wayland, 1999)

Reynoldson, Fiona, *The Past in Pictures: The Home Front* (Wayland, 1999)

Reynoldson, Fiona, *What Families Were Like: The Second World War* (Hodder Wayland, 2002)

Websites

BBC WW2 People's War. An archive of people's memories of World War Two: http://www.bbc.co.uk/dna/ww2/

Fun interactive BBC site, in which you can pretend to go shopping in wartime Britain, read letters from evacuees and hear the sound of an air-raid warning: http://www.bbc.co.uk/history/ww2children//index.shtml

Home Sweet Home Front site containing useful information, and interesting photos and posters on various key topics: rationing, Dig for Victory, land girls, evacuees, squander: http://www.homesweethomefront.co.uk/templates/hshf_frameset_tem.htm

The Second World War Experience Centre site, with descriptions of aspects of life on the home front, and memories from those who experienced it: http://www.war-experience.org/history/keyaspects/home-british/

The Home Front section of the Spartacus Second World War Encyclopedia: http://www.spartacus.schoolnet.co.uk/2WWhome.htm

Wartime Memories Project. An interactive site containing questions to and answers from people who lived through World War Two: http://www.wartimememories.co.uk/questions.html

Note to parents and teachers

Every effort has been made by the Publishers to ensure that these websites are suitable for children; that they are of the highest educational value, and that they contain no inappropriate or offensive material. However, because of the nature of the Internet, it is impossible to guarantee that the contents of these sites will not be altered. We strongly advise that Internet access is supervised by a responsible adult.

INDEX

Thanks to the following for permission to quote from their sources: (pp. 9, 13, 25, 29) BBC WW2 People's War website; (p. 17) *Mr Brown's War, A Diary of the Second World War*, edited by Helen D Millgate, Sutton Publishing.